Standing in the ghostly moonlight of the plains, the sentinel in Frederic Remington's painting watches for Indians and buffalo with his rifle cocked.

COVER: *The howling fury of Indians attacking a wagon train and the sudden death of both Indians and settlers fills this 1854 canvas of Charles Wimar.*

FRONT ENDSHEET: *The Great Emigration of 1843 sent a wave of pioneers west. Albert Bierstadt painted this view of one caravan nearing its destination.*

CONTENTS PAGE: *A war party, painted by George Catlin, carrying hatchets and decorated shields, moves Indian-file across the wide and barren plains.*

BACK ENDSHEET: *Cries and shouts fill the air as a war party rides around camp at the climax of its ceremonial preparation for battle with the enemy.*

*"A knowledge of the past prepares us for the crisis
of the present and the challenge of the future."*

JOHN F. KENNEDY
From his special foreword in Volume 1

THE AMERICAN HERITAGE
NEW ILLUSTRATED HISTORY
OF THE UNITED STATES

VOLUME 6

THE FRONTIER

By ROBERT G. ATHEARN
Professor of History, University of Colorado

CREATED AND DESIGNED BY THE EDITORS OF
AMERICAN HERITAGE
The Magazine of History

PUBLISHED BY
DELL PUBLISHING CO., INC., NEW YORK

CONTENTS OF THE COMPLETE SERIES

Foreword by JOHN F. KENNEDY
Introduction by ALLAN NEVINS
Main text by ROBERT G. ATHEARN

A MASTER INDEX FOR ALL 16 VOLUMES APPEARS IN VOLUME 16

CONTENTS OF VOLUME 6

CHAPTER 16

Moving West

By the Treaty of 1783 that ended the Revolution, the western boundary of the new nation was the Mississippi River. The settlers, no longer restricted by officials in London, immediately began to migrate in large numbers into the regions beyond the Appalachians. Their curiosity was the same as that of the early promoter who once asked of the Carolina frontier, "If the Porch be so beautiful, what must the Temple be?" Up to the War of 1812, the invasion of the Ohio River country and the land beyond was held partially in check by Indian opposition. The war broke the Indians' resistance, and after its conclusion, the defeated natives were forced back and the big land rush was on.

The westward movement is often considered in terms of a "frontier line" that progressed inexorably toward the Pacific Ocean. This artificial marker designated the boundary between the country having more than two people per square mile and that

Daniel Boone was the most famous of the pioneers of the Old Southwest. This print is from Chester Harding's 1819 portrait.

having fewer. In 1790, this line could have been found as far east as the Atlantic Ocean in parts of Maine. It skirted through Vermont, New Hampshire, eastern New York, eastern Pennsylvania, down through Virginia, and into the Carolinas. Of the 4,000,000 people living in the United States at that time, 94% were east of such a frontier line. By 1860, the same line ran through Wisconsin, Minnesota, Iowa, Nebraska, Kansas, and into Texas. By that time, too, another frontier line, across the Great Plains, had made an eastward indentation in California and Oregon on the Pacific Coast. The census taker of 1860 discovered there were then 31,500,000 people in the country, with about half of them living west of the Appalachians. California could claim more people in its decade as a state than New Hampshire had collected in all its history.

What were the reasons for such a growth? The chief inducement to the Western settler was cheap land. Those in the East, who saw available land disappear and prices rise, looked thoughtfully to the West, where land was not only more fertile but much cheaper. Europeans also looked enviously toward Western America. In their part of the world, the soil had been worked for centuries. It was not common, furthermore, for the individual in the Old World to be able to own his own farm. Usually he was a tenant. The existence of limitless, inexpensive acres on the American frontiers was a powerful attraction to prospective immigrants. Further encouragement came from the belief that individual opportunity and freedom were greater under the democratic form of government. While this alone may not have been enough to induce a man to move, it perhaps helped him to make his decision as he thought about owning a farm of his own in the American West.

Before 1862, land was not free, but until then it had always been relatively low-priced. Under the Ordinance of 1785, the federal domain was to be divided into townships six miles square, each of them subdivided into 640-acre sections, one mile square. Sale was by auction, at $1 per acre, a difficult system for the small buyer. In 1796, a provision was made for credit, but the price was raised to $2 per acre. Although Easterners thought this reasonable, it was too expensive for many frontiersmen. Loud complaints brought another change in 1800. Now the farmer could buy as few as 320 acres, and land offices were set up closer to the Western tracts. But the price was not lowered. Agitation continued until the minimum size

of farms was again reduced and the price was cut. The new law of 1820 allowed a man to buy as few as 80 acres at $1.25 per acre. This meant that $100 would buy a farm. It also indicated that the government policy had shifted from one of trying to make money from the public domain to one that emphasized locating farmers on the land. Yet a cash payment of $100 was still a burden to the pioneer, and most Western lands continued to be bought for speculation rather than settlement.

In 1841, another concession was given to the land-hungry. The Preemption Act provided that a man could settle upon land not yet opened for sale and still have the first chance at his own tract when surveys were made. In other words, "squatting" was legalized. Then, in 1862, the Homestead Act offered a quarter section of 160 acres free to a person who would settle and make certain improvements. Any adult citizen, or adult person declaring his intention to become a citizen, was eligible. It is small wonder that thousands of people in Europe and America began to think of pulling up stakes and heading west.

Establishing a new home in the West was not as easy as it appeared, however. The encouragements were great, but practical difficulties stood in the way. The main barrier, particularly during the early years of American experience, was a lack of adequate transportation. Roads were few, and those in existence were usu-

Two early settlers, on the trail with their covered wagons, try to yoke an ox that struggles to elude them, in a scene painted by William Henry Jackson.

ally wretched. Until the decade of the 1850s, there were also few railroads west of the Appalachians, and they were of little value to the settler. The best avenues of transportation, before the day of the canals and railroads, were the Ohio and Mississippi Rivers and their many tributaries. The Great Lakes, of course, had long been used in the westward movement.

It is true that a pioneer family, given enough time, could work its way across an unfriendly land to settle in some remote spot. But that did not solve a problem; it created one. Far from markets, the settler had no easy way to sell his agricultural products, unless he could use the rivers. But not every farm was near a navigable stream. This meant that the farmer was often forced to use up his own produce, and in such circumstances he was not likely to raise much more than his family required. Such "subsistence" living was severely limiting.

The situation presented by the Indian was also significant. From the outset, the natives were disturbed by the growing number of whites and by their hunger for land. The inevitable clash lasted from the time of the Pequot War in New England in 1637 to the final battles on the Great Plains and in the Southwest near the close of the 19th century. The whites had on their side the advantage of numbers and the superior weapons of an industrialized nation, but at

One of the many shiploads of 19th-century Irish immigrants fleeing the potato famine debarks at New York City. In the harbor is the Keying, *which claimed to be the first Chinese ship to visit America.*

times they had a two-front problem. Ahead were resisting Indians, and behind on occasion were governments that tried to restrain their encroachments on the natives' lands. How the whites overran the continent is not a pretty story. It is one of deceit, of cruelty on both sides, of lawbreaking, and of the final triumph of a stronger people. Today sympathies are largely with the Indians, but that is not much consolation to the dispossessed.

Another obstacle to westward expansion was financial. Then, as now, it took money to move a family. Before 1862, land cost $1.25 an acre, and, even supposing a satisfactory farm could be had for that figure, additional funds were needed to pay expenses until the first crop could be harvested. Moreover, the frontier was a place of speculation and inflation. The result was often a roller-coaster economy that climbed to great heights and then plunged in violent descents. When financial panics came—as they did in 1819 and 1837—the severest kind of depressions staggered the Western economy. Many pioneer families were driven back to the East, bankrupt and thoroughly disheartened. Where instability was worst, whole communities were virtually wiped out, and the frontier line was halted until the settlers' forces could

gather strength for a fresh assault.

Despite all discouragements, the westward movement persisted. Its main body was resolute farmers who accustomed themselves to privation and suffering, whether from isolation, Indians, or monetary fluctuation. They came from New England, whose changing economy and thin topsoil drove them to search for new and better land. Southerners, faced by increasing competition from large, slaveholding landowners, moved west in search of a more favorable competitive situation. Europeans, tired of political turmoil and economic disruptions, joined the westward-moving

agrarian army. So great was the influx that one prominent New York merchant was moved to complain, "All Europe is coming across the ocean—all that part at least who cannot make a living at home—and what shall we do with them?" He need not have been worried, for at that time—during the 1830s—few of the newcomers tarried long in the Eastern port cities. The magnetic attraction of land drew them on, through the mountain passes, down the slopes of the Appalachians, and out toward the great Mississippi Valley.

The new West welcomed these strangers. Young states, eager for growth and political importance, employed immigration commissioners whose business it was to publicize their part of the country. Thousands of pamphlets poured out of their offices, printed in different European languages. The smallest villages in Germany, Ireland, Switzerland, and Scandinavia became acquainted with economic possibilities in remote places like Wisconsin, Illinois, and Indiana. By 1860, the census revealed that the percentage of aliens in the state of Wisconsin was larger than that of Eastern districts and that a goodly number of Eastern-born people had moved to Western homes—a fact that disturbed Atlantic-seaboard communities whose population was being drained away. Vermonters, for example, noticed that while their population stood almost still, such upstart areas as Iowa grew by more than 250% during the 1850s.

Western life

Isolation from the Atlantic seaboard tended to make Westerners look to the South. Those along the Ohio and Mississippi Rivers regarded New Orleans as their chief market, for it was no great task to build crude plank flatboats upon which farmers could float downriver with tons of produce. There they sold their crops, knocked apart the flatboats, sold the planks, and returned home. This commercial necessity early gave the West, from Minnesota to Louisiana, a unity that only the Civil War would disrupt.

Distance from market, and distance from one's neighbors, had the effect of continuing and even magnifying the earlier-developed characteristics of independence and self-reliance. The farther west the frontier moved, and the more remote its settlements, the greater was its tendency to mold men who were not only self-sustaining but

often strong-willed about conducting their affairs as they saw fit. Thus isolation, although it presented problems, also shaped a society whose ideas and practices affected later generations of Westerners as well as the nation itself.

Until the frontier farmer reached the prairies of Minnesota and Iowa, he was obliged to spend most of his time clearing trees from the land in order to plant his crops. Agricultural life must often have seemed a nightmare of blackened stumps that defied the plow. So tree-conscious did the farmer become that when he emerged from the wooded regions and came upon open patches of land, he could not believe that the soil was as good as that of the forested lands. Yet when he left behind the timbered country and moved onto the rolling, treeless prairies of the West, he discovered that the tree had not been without its virtues. Now he remembered that it had supplied him with many of his necessities. Split-rail fences, log houses, pole-lined walls—indeed, the old oaken bucket itself—had come from his groves. So had his benches, tables, beds, floors, and even his clay-lined log fireplace. Fuel for fires had never been a problem to him before. Now he faced a country without wood.

Wherever the frontiersman lived, he was also burdened with the problem of defense. Normally he provided his own. Government—national, state, or county—was traditionally unable to give adequate protection against the resentful Indians. Nor could government always control lawless whites, especially where the countryside was thinly populated. Many pioneer agrarians worked at their daily tasks encumbered by their heavy rifles.

In the beginning, Western justice was necessarily swift and violent. Men solved legal problems directly and in an individual way. Their code was somewhat different from ours, but it developed out of the exigencies

Drifting down with the river's current is a loaded flatboat, and pushing its way up the river is what replaced it as a carrier of cargo, the great steamboat.

461

The frontier created powerful and fantastic folk heroes who fitted its incredible characteristics, like this boatman driving two harnessed water monsters.

of the time. To understand why sudden death was the penalty for horse-stealing, one must remember that loss of a horse might mean mortal danger to its owner. Men were punished by floggings and banishment because communities often did not have jails and penitentiaries.

Because the frontier was essentially agricultural, day-to-day existence was generally drab and uninteresting. It was a life of dawn-to-dusk work ridding the fields of timber and rocks, sowing, cultivating, and harvesting crops, and getting a bare livelihood in return. Little time or energy remained for pursuits of the mind. Men's values tended to be more practical and mate-

Timber cleared from the land was used in many ways, as material for the split-rail fence and as lumber for the log cabin.

rial. In religion, frontier families wanted exhilaration rather than contemplation. Understandably, the revival movement captured their attention and interest, for they could appreciate both its direct approach and its action.

Despite their long hours of labor, the frontier people did not altogether ignore the cultural side of life. But they did not have much opportunity to make original contributions to native literature, drama, or music. Except for occasional folk music, about all they could do was mimic the East and try to reproduce its civilization as they knew it. They were conscious of their deficiencies, yet the slightest inference of any cultural lag aroused instant animosity.

Perhaps the Westerners' realization of their cultural isolation explains

Women's seminaries were in existence by the early 1800s. Here, at graduation exercises, a wreath is placed on the head of one of the honor students.

their efforts to compensate. Great value was attached to books, and no small amount of respect was given to those with "book learning," although this feeling was kept well hidden. A surprising number of log homes had copies of *Pilgrim's Progress* and other classic works. The family Bible was treasured as literature as well as a family archive where births and deaths were recorded. Newspapers and almanacs also were found in many homes. Villages tried—and often failed—to support local newspapers, for they were the chief mediums of intellectual communication on the frontier.

Most Westerners privately admitted that an education was a worthy and desirable achievement, but to gain it was both difficult and expensive. The common man had to content himself with the most rudimentary kind of learning. A minimum acquaintance with the basic "three Rs" sufficed to carry on what simple business transactions confronted him, and there was little necessity to rise above this level. When children had learned to read, write, and do simple arithmetic, there was a tendency to take them from the classroom and put them to some of the many tasks required by a growing economy. More extended education was often opposed on the ground that it was too costly in time and money. Private schools struggled against this attitude, and even public schools, praised as a matter of policy, were damned because they increased taxes. Sometimes higher education received attention only because church organizations were willing to appropriate money for the construction and maintenance of buildings. But even these efforts did not serve many students. Before 1800, Transylvania University at Lexington, Kentucky, was the only institution of higher learning west of the Appalachians, and its struggle for existence was nothing short of heroic. To the Westerner, learning was a laudable achievement, but he viewed it as a social frill to be added only after the fulfillment of the family's material needs.

As people of an area characterized by hard physical labor, frontiersmen quickly became scornful of those who did not work with their hands. Even the preacher and the teacher took their turns at manual labor and thereby found a place in the hearts of their neighbors. There were, of course, practical reasons for this participation, for there was not enough labor in most Western communities to support nonproducers. In the hardworking, isolated society there also developed a general disdain for Europeans, who seemed to be regarded by Westerners as aristocrats and snobs. This rejection of the old country helped mold the newcomers into a breed that became even more anti-European than the residents of the Atlantic seaboard. So strong was the feeling that it became a part of the American heritage.

When the United States won its freedom from Great Britain, it faced a number of difficult problems. One was administering Western lands that had not yet been organized into states. Americans, who had just ended their successful fight against the British colonial system, did not regard their Western possessions as colonies. But when the new nation chose to govern those lands from Washington, even through appointed "territorial" governors, judges, and other officials, many frontiersmen saw a parallel to the British imperial policy and protested vehemently.

Uncle Sam's stepchildren

There was one outstanding difference between the two systems. The Northwest Ordinance of 1787, enacted even before the writing of the Constitution, set at rest some of the fears that the federal Congress would forever withhold self-government from parts of the nation. It said a territory could enter the Union upon fulfilling certain requirements. When its free adult male population reached 5,000, it could elect a legislature. It could send to Congress a delegate who could make speeches, but could not vote. When its population reached 60,000 free inhabitants, application for statehood could be made.

Despite the promise of eventual statehood, guaranteed again when the Constitution was adopted, many fron-

Fort Snelling, Minnesota, painted by the soldier-artist Seth Eastman in the 1840s, was for more than 30 years the army's farthest Northwest outpost.

tiersmen felt that their pre-Revolution problems were not wholly solved. Each new westward wave of people put the outer edge of civilization farther from the central government at Washington. As the distance grew, so did a feeling of resentment toward those who governed from afar. Complaints against appointed officials were frequent. The federal army, charged with the task of protecting remote settlements against the Indians, was subject to bitter criticism for its short-comings. It was easy for those engaged in pioneering to believe they were political stepchildren, neglected and forgotten by a self-indulgent parent.

The most important result of this attitude was the inclination of territorial residents to shift for themselves, just as the colonials had during England's period of "salutary neglect." When the army failed to live up to expectations in punishing marauding Indians, Westerners went into action.

Volunteers, led by governors who were often ambitious politicians in search of fame, took to the field to eliminate the Indian enemy. Sometimes this led to warfare of such proportions that federal help was needed to restore peace, but the territorial people looked upon this simply as evidence of the government's original laxity.

Westerners were also likely to take political matters into their own hands. During the 1770s, some of them set up a local government along Tennessee's Watauga River and went into business for themselves. Formulating Articles of Association, they elected 13 representatives, who in turn appointed five commissioners to operate the new government. It was as spontaneous as the Mayflower Compact 150 years earlier. It was a body politic, born full-grown, ready and able to govern itself. Three-quarters of a century later, in 1859, Colorado miners would organize miniature governments in

Vigilante headquarters in San Francisco in 1856 was called Fort Gunnybags because of its fortifications. Note the accusing eye on the official seal.

467

mining camps yet untouched by the long arm of Eastern law. The propensity to write constitutions and set up governments ran strong among the frontiersmen. They were a great do-it-yourself people.

Significance of the frontier

Before the Mexican War, the country called the West extended from the Appalachian Mountains to a line not far across the Mississippi River. This was the area of settlement and of agricultural development. The land beyond was vaguely called the Far West. It was the haunt of the Indian, the trapper, and the occasional explorer. Economically, it was not yet significant. By the Louisiana Purchase of 1803, the United States acquired the remote reaches between the Mississippi and the Rockies, but little could be done at once to develop that territory. The nation was not ready.

Although settlement of the Western plains was delayed, the region we call the Midwest was rapidly populated between 1815 and the 1840s. Migration into this region had important influences upon the nation at large. It provided a growing market for Eastern manufactures and encouraged the rising industrial areas to develop all possible means of transportation to and from the West. Both influences were accelerated when settlers moved onto the treeless plains, where they required outside help to get fencing, lumber, furniture, and hardware. Once the farmer moved to where he could market his crops for cash, his dependence upon manufactures grew fast. He became highly important to Eastern businessmen, who regarded him as a prime prospect.

Socially, the great advance of settlement had the effect of increasing the Americanization process typical of the frontier. As the leveling influence touched larger numbers, the nation felt its effect, for by now the West was much more powerful in Congress. Western members thundered their ideologies throughout legislative halls, and the "little people" the length and breadth of the land listened. Thus the social influences of the frontier had their effect upon political growth. The common man, wherever he was, came to demand a greater share in government, and during the Jackson era in particular the movement reached epic proportions.

Finally, the growth of the Mississippi and Ohio River Valleys set the scene for the next big move westward. It provided a training ground for those who would go on. Although some adjustments had to be made for the assault upon a new kind of land, where agricultural practices would have to be modified, it was a good place to learn the trade. The nation at large looked on and approved of such successful expansion. When the day came for Americans to make the great leap across the plains to Oregon and California, they would be ready, for by then "westering" had become a part of the national tradition.

KNOEDLER GALLERIES

THE GREAT GOLD RUSH

January 24, 1848, when James Marshall found gold in the race of the sawmill he was building for John Sutter, is an important date in the history of California and the West. This chance discovery was to set off the biggest and the gaudiest gold rush ever—and, ironically, was to leave both Marshall and Sutter broke at the end of their lives. Sutter, fearing that his land would be overrun when word of the discovery was circulated, did his best to hush up the news and keep miners away. At first many *were* skeptical, not realizing the extent of the bonanza. Then, in May, a huckstering genius named Sam Brannan —a Mormon businessman who saw a chance to make a fortune by building a store for the miners near Sutter's mill—appeared in San Francisco, waving a bottle full of gold dust and shouting, "Gold! Gold from the American River!" His electrifying performance produced a frenzy. In about a week, crowds of people began to go to Sutter's mill. San Francisco became, for a time, a ghost town, and as word spread, thousands flocked to the gold fields from every part of the world. The great gold rush was on, and the lust to get rich quick consumed the minds of men from all walks of life. Typical of the many who sought gold is the quartet above, using both a pan and a cradle.

JOHN AUGUSTUS SUTTER

GOLD! GOLD! GOLD!

It was at John Sutter's sawmill (below), on the bank of the American River at Coloma, that his building foreman, James Marshall, first discovered gold.

When the gold rush began, the trading post at Sutter's Fort (above) was the center of John Sutter's private empire. As gold seekers swarmed over his land, and his help ran away to the diggings, his holdings vanished. But Sam Brannan, who had proclaimed the discovery, became a rich man.

JAMES MARSHALL
CALIFORNIA STATE LIBRARY

SAM BRANNAN
CALIFORNIA HISTORICAL SOCIETY

The famous nugget that Marshall took from Sutter's mill is actually only dime-size.

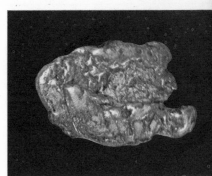

UNIVERSITY OF CALIFORNIA

471

THE GREAT GOLD RUSH

CALIFORNIA, HERE THEY COME!

The frantic pursuit of gold is mocked by N. Currier in this 1849 print with the title, *The Way They Go to California*. The prospectors (right) scream for places on steamers and more fantastic conveyances like the rocket and balloon.

HOW THEY MINED GOLD

LOS ANGELES COUNTY MUSEUM

This prospector is using a washbowl, or pan, to take gold out of the sand of a creek bed. The principle of gold panning depends on the fact that gold is about eight times as heavy as sand and will sink to the bottom of the pan while the lighter sand is spilled over the edge by the water. The process was inefficient and many flakes of gold were lost.

Because group ventures had more chance of success, the day of the individual miner soon passed. In the daguerreotype above, six men operate a gravel-washing machine called a cradle. Such devices could handle far greater amounts of gold-bearing dirt than a miner with a pan.

The Long Tom (right) was a trough with a piece of perforated sheet iron at one end. Water from a stream ran through constantly, washing the dirt that was shoveled in. Cleats in a "ripple box" underneath the iron sheet then caught the heavy flakes of gold as they settled.

OVERLEAF: The larger the gravel-washing machines became, the more water their operation required. Groups of miners often cooperated to build systems of water wheels like this one at Cut Eye Foster's Bar on the North Yuba River in California that supplied water for Long Toms.

HARSH JUSTICE

As there was often no one to protect them from robbery and violence, gold seekers were moved to take the law into their own hands. In the painting above, an accused horse thief (standing, center, in long coat) is tried in a miner's cabin.

The forty-niner who would rather steal his gold than dig for it is caricatured at the left. Such men were dealt with harshly. In the miners' courts, the penalties ranged from hanging for the large thefts and murder to flogging for petty crimes.

Joaquin Murietta (right) terrorized California during the gold rush with a series of murders, stagecoach holdups, and cattle thefts. After he was killed in 1853, his head was exhibited in a bottle.

THE GREAT GOLD RUSH

IT WAS NOT ALL WORK

Hangtown (above, left)—or Placerville, as it is now known—acquired its unsavory name when three robbers were strung up from a tree in its main street. One of many gold-rush boom towns, it was once California's third-largest settlement.

The absence of women in remote mining camps did not prevent forty-niners from holding an occasional fandango, like the abandoned affair above. "Ladies" were designated by a patch on their pants or a handkerchief worn on their sleeves.

Sunday was for some a time of rest and contemplation; for others an excuse to continue Saturday night's binge. In the painting at the left, a brawl erupts, a horse race is run, and a miner celebrates a strike. The men in the center write home or listen to a Bible reading. At the right, a miner washes what remains of his pants.

481

COLLECTION OF ROBERT HONEYMAN

THE GREAT GOLD RUSH

MEN
WITHOUT
WOMEN

NEW-YORK HISTORICAL SOCIETY

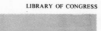

"Married, Mum?" is the question women-starved prospectors are asking a pretty young lady who has just arrived in their mining camp, in the German lithograph at the left, above. At the right she gives her encouraging and well-received reply: "No, sir!" The dancing girl (above, far right) traveled with one of the many vaudeville shows that had become a regular fixture in the gold fields by the late 1850s.

Men of many nations sought their fortunes in California. At the left, Mexican rancheros, American miners, and Chinese laborers mingle in a San Francisco bar.

Away from the pleasures (and restraints) of wife and family, gold seekers often sought solace in the saloon. At the right, three prospectors enjoy a friendly nip.

483

A BOOM TOWN'S PROGRESS

NEW-YORK HISTORICAL SOCIETY

As prospectors poured into California, new towns appeared by the score. None grew with greater abandon than bawdy San Francisco, the port city that was the gateway to the mining country. When the influx began, the one-time Spanish settlement was so unprepared for it that hundreds had to camp in tents on Telegraph Hill (above). While buildings went up, the streets (left) remained a morass of mud. But by the 1860s, when the daguerreotype at the right was taken, the city had little resemblance to the village of 800 people that it had been just before the gold rush.

CHAPTER 17

CRUSADES AND CULTURE

The nation's physical expansion during the years that followed the War of 1812 had a deeper meaning than merely an increase of population and industrial development. As the American people witnessed a growing economic independence from Great Britain and Europe, and counted the new Western states entering the Union, they experienced a swelling pride in what the world called the great democratic experiment. To the national structure, they now wished to add some of the refinements of society without which the job could not be regarded as properly finished.

The large cities grew along the East Coast, and for a long time theaters, libraries, schools, and other evidences of cultural interest and support were centered there. Westerners, absorbed in carving out an empire, and necessarily concerned with the day-to-day problems of living, were at first inclined to jeer at Eastern cultural efforts. This was merely an admission of their own shortcomings. As soon as

New York's Park Theatre in 1829 had no rule against wearing hats or standing in the orchestra. But ladies sat upstairs.

possible, they tried to acquire some of the refinements of life for themselves, usually copying their Eastern brothers. Most of the plays and concerts in the West were imported from the East or from Europe. Only when Western communities had passed the frontier stage did any native talent emerge.

Accompanying the intellectual ferment and increased democratization of the first half of the 19th century was a strong humanitarian surge. Suddenly America found itself fascinated by reform in every part of life. The movement had some of its roots in a revulsion against the evils revealed in industrial England, where labor, depressed and discontented, began to react violently. As yet, America had not developed a proletariat—a propertyless working class—of any size. Nevertheless, its factory system already had begun to breed social inequalities to which believers in Jacksonian democracy objected. In an era when the rights of man were so greatly stressed, anyone with a grievance against the more entrenched members of the established order found listeners.

The emphasis of reform, however, was not upon the plight of the working class. That would have been an admission of guilt by factory owners, and even in this early day the public believed that industrial development must in no way be disturbed. Businessmen were willing to lend a sympathetic ear to the woes of the underprivileged, as long as their troubles were not associated with the conditions of their employment. Reformers were directed to other fertile fields, such as the improvement of conditions among the blind, deaf, insane, poor, and imprisoned.

Humanitarian impulses

Pauperism was one of the economic ills that required attention. In a land of plenty it had no justifiable place. Also, the pauper's prison was an inheritance from England that now came to be regarded as unwelcome and un-American. Many states abolished imprisonment for debt. City fathers of rising industrial towns were moved to provide breadlines and other charitable aids in the face of growing unevenness of employment. They saw the alternative as one of violence if the workers were pushed too far, and they responded as much

This actionful lithograph shows Jennie Lind, "The Swedish Nightingale," sleighing past P.T. Barnum's American Museum in New York City. It was Barnum, the great promoter of the unusual, who brought the famous soprano to America for the first time in 1850, and she was a tremendous success. She had clothing, furniture, and even a clipper ship named after her.

out of fear as out of philanthropy. That they acted at all is perhaps to their credit.

The lot of other unfortunates was considerably alleviated during these years. As the nation became larger and its law-enforcement agencies improved, prisons grew crowded. There was a recognized need for the improvement of conditions in public institutions, as well as for the reclassification of persons who were arrested. For years paupers, the insane, petty offenders, and professional criminals had been thrown together indiscriminately. New institutions were established for the mentally ill, the blind, the deaf, and for others who were handicapped. There was also an increasing tendency to regard them as wards of the state, rather than to rely upon the uncertain efforts of private charities or allow those needing care or treatment to stay with their families, who were often unable to meet their needs.

One of the oldest and most persistent American crusades for reform was the temperance movement. There were hundreds of local societies as early as the 1830s, and during that decade a national organization called the United States Temperance Union appeared. Some of the groups had odd origins. One was the Washingtonians, whose fighting core sprang from a small number of alcoholics in Baltimore. One night in 1840, the revelers staggered into a temperance meeting in that city and were so im-

"Father, come home," pleads a child in Ten Nights in a Barroom, *a novel that won converts for temperance in the 1850s.*

pressed by the earnestness of the reformers that they retreated to a tavern and founded a new temperance society. Taking the name of the country's first President, they dedicated themselves to alcoholic moderation. The initiation fee was set at 25¢, and monthly dues at half that figure. A few years later, the society published the *Washingtonian Teetotaler's Minstrel,* a songbook that contained such deathless classics as *Dear Father, Drink No More* and *Mother, Dry That*

Flowing Tear. Most famous of the temperance books, however, was Timothy Shay Arthur's *Ten Nights in a Barroom,* published in 1854. It was adapted for dramatic presentation and came near rivaling *Uncle Tom's Cabin* for sustained popularity.

Another part of the reform movement—one regarded with little enthusiasm by the male population—was the demand by women for equality. Since the days of Benjamin Franklin and Thomas Paine, a few intellectuals had taken the position that the shackles of tradition, rather than a natural mental inferiority, kept women in a secondary position. Such notions were regarded by the masculine majority as much too advanced, if not downright dangerous. They insisted that woman's place was in the home, away from public view, and that her first jobs were domestic duties and child-bearing.

During the second quarter of the 19th century, the voice of womanhood was loud in the general outcry against special privilege. Although the women heard from were a small minority, their complaints echoed across the land. One militant feminist, Amelia Bloomer, who edited a temperance reform journal called *The Lily,* sought to dramatize her demand for equality by wearing mannish attire. She appeared in public in a short overskirt, reaching only to the unmentionable region of the knee, with pantaloons tied discreetly at the ankles to cover her lower extremities. Naturally, it caused a sensation. Elizabeth Cady Stanton, another of the feminine progressives, adopted a similar outfit and wore it in the face of considerable derision from street urchins who followed her about, chanting uncomplimentary doggerel.

By verbal bombardment and public nagging the women made some progress. John Greenleaf Whittier and Ralph Waldo Emerson of the literary world, and Wendell Phillips and William Lloyd Garrison, prominent abolitionists, came to their support. Even Abraham Lincoln, a young politician out in Illinois, declared he had no objection to sharing government with women. Before long some of the states began to relax their laws, permitting women to hold property and to be freed of liability for their husbands' debts. As a dividend, the movement produced a greater interest in the rights of children, whose increasing exploitation in factories was becoming a matter of national concern.

The antislavery crusade

Climaxing the humanitarian movements of the period was the crusade against human slavery. By the early 19th century, there was an increasing feeling through most of the country that something ought to be done to check the spread of what was generally regarded as an evil.

When the American Colonization Society was founded in 1816 to relocate Negroes abroad, it found support among humanitarians in both North and South. John Randolph of Virginia and William H. Crawford, another prominent Southerner, were active in it. At one time Henry Clay of Kentucky was its president. Although the society did not succeed in sending any appreciable number of slaves out of the country, or cope with the fundamental problem of Negro freedom, its existence tended for a time to satisfy the more moderate antislave groups. By the 1830s, interest in the abolition of slavery had sharply declined across the cotton belt, but in the North, particularly in New England, the movement was beginning to rise to the peak it would reach in the Civil War.

There were two reasons for a shift in Southern attitudes toward slavery. First, as new Southwestern lands were opened to growing cotton, the institution became more profitable to plantation owners. With the world price of cotton maintaining high levels and with an increasing availability of cotton-growing land, the Southerner found more use for Negro labor than he had at an earlier time. The second reason for a stiffening defense of slavery was the extreme abolitionist stand taken by a small group of Northern crusaders. Their attitude that all slaveholders were moral lepers deeply angered Southerners, whether or not they owned slaves. This response, partly psychological, stemmed from the South's agrarian tradition, which was pastoral and antimercantile. Many Southerners feared that if they abandoned slavery, they themselves would become slaves of Northeastern industrial capitalism.

As in all great crusades, leadership was provided by tough-minded, outspoken individuals wholly dedicated to the cause. William Lloyd Garrison was typical. The young man first came to notice as an employee of Benjamin Lundy, publisher of a Baltimore abolitionist journal. Put in jail for printing libelous statements, Garrison stayed there seven weeks before being bailed out by a wealthy philanthropist. Thoroughly aroused, the newly freed printer hastened to Boston, where he started his own paper, *The Liberator.* In its first issue, January 1, 1831, Garrison took his stand, from which he never wavered. Contending that he did not wish to think, speak, or write with moderation upon the subject of abolition, he declared angrily, "I am in earnest—I will not equivocate—I will not excuse—I will not retreat a single inch—and *I will be heard.*" He called the Constitution "a covenant with death and an agreement with hell," and swore that he would rather see the Union destroyed than to see it countenance the institution of slavery.

Garrison's literary blasts got attention from both supporters and enemies, but it was Theodore Weld, working in the Midwest, who made the most converts. His followers got many of their beliefs from the religious revivals of Charles G. Finney during the 1820s, and now, led by Weld, the group emphasized the religious-moral aspect of slavery, holding the institution to be a moral sin. Weld had more skill than Garrison in both organizing and publicizing. Whereas Garrison often antagonized prospective converts, Weld was more persuasive, even extending his efforts to Congress, where he helped to form an antislavery bloc. Many of the young reformer's followers were students at Oberlin College, founded in Ohio in 1833. It was one of the first American institutions of higher learning to admit Negroes and was also the first to admit women, in 1835. Modern studies have shown that Weld probably accomplished as much for his cause as the dogmatic Garrison did.

It was not unnatural that such a controversial issue should make its way into politics. In 1840, its adherents formed the Liberty Party and nominated James G. Birney, an abolitionist writer, for President. But in the national election, Birney got only slightly more than 7,000 votes, mostly in New England. Considering the general hostility to abolitionist extremism, it is perhaps surprising that he did that well. In time, however, increasing numbers of Northerners convinced themselves that the aristocratic masters of the South should be curbed, and the trend to vote against these political Bourbons grew. The important point of the antislavery crusade is that the feelings it aroused mounted steadily until it had gained a significant number of followers. By the time Lincoln ran for the Presi-

Amelia Bloomer and her followers, who wanted equal rights for women, advocated a more mannish style of costume. It caused ridicule, but its full trousers gave the word "bloomers" to the language.

493

Public schools were generally accepted by the mid-19th century, and the teacher of that time was allowed to use the rod liberally in educating the student.

dency, the crusade against "social evils" was a potent political weapon.

The little red schoolhouse

Along with improved conditions among men and women of all classes came more interest in education. Particular emphasis was put on free education—a principle not as readily approved as modern students might suppose. But by the mid-19th century, state-supported schools were generally accepted, especially in the North and West. Children of the wealthy were still likely to be found in private schools, but it was no longer a mark of financial inability if one's children attended public institutions.

The explanation for the wide acceptance of public education is found in the determined crusade of those who believed in its virtues. Representative of those who felt strongly was a youthful Michigan judge who, as early as 1806, urged the creation of a public school system in that new territory. He argued that it would "advance the future prosperity of the country and the happiness of millions yet unborn." Hundreds of other far-seeing Americans whose names are forgotten gave support to this part of the nation's further democratization. As in all movements, some individuals stood out. Horace Mann devoted a lifetime to the improvement of educational facilities and the expansion of the school curriculum. The inclusion of such subjects as music and hygiene was met with stubborn opposition by those who thought the young were unnecessarily pampered.

Henry Barnard was another leader in the field. He was instrumental in establishing the first state teachers' association, in 1845, and in the founding of the *American Journal of Education.* Later he helped to start the University of Wisconsin.

Literary growth

Before 1815, a good part of the literature read in this country was produced in England. Haughtily a British journal of 1820 asked the unkind question, "In the four quarters of the globe, who reads an American book?" Often the books published on this side of the Atlantic were pirated editions of English works. Charles Dickens was only one of the Victorian writers who strongly protested our refusal to recognize British copyright laws and the consequent loss of royalties to authors.

As part of their general declaration of independence, Americans eventually began to write and publish their own books. James Fenimore Cooper was said to have written his first novel, in 1820, as the result of a boast that he could turn out a better book than the English product he was reading. He determined to write a strictly American story. In *The Spy* he was eminently successful. His depiction of the American Indian in the *Leatherstocking Tales* deeply impressed Europeans, who regarded our natives as examples of Rousseau's man of nature, the *beau savage.* The sentimentally idealized Cooper Indian became so fixed in the minds of readers that the image is still with us today. The Lone Ranger's Tonto and Red Ryder's Little Beaver are modern examples of the type.

A few years after Cooper began writing, Ralph Waldo Emerson underscored the trend toward a native literature when he commented, "Let us have done with Europe and dead cultures, let us explore the possibilities of our own new world." Emerson, Henry David Thoreau, and a number of others including Orestes Brownson, Margaret Fuller, Theodore Parker, Bronson Alcott, and George Bancroft created a school of literature and thought known as Transcendentalism. They believed that moral law transcended natural law, that the knowledge of truth—implanted by God—transcended experience and reason. Their beliefs helped them to justify in their own minds the ideal of individual freedom—something rather easy for the inheritors of New England Puritanism with its faith in man's capacity for personal spiritual insight. Out of this school came a torrent of writing critical of an America that, to the Transcendentalists, was not living up to its potentialities. A tangible example of their belief was the establishment of Brook Farm in Massachusetts, one of a number of experiments in community living.

The social and intellectual stirrings, so apparent during the years that followed our second war with Great Britain, were indications of an emerging American nationality. Not only were we issuing declarations of independence—some of them perhaps unconsciously—in all aspects of daily life, but we were also turning our backs on Europe, determined to show the world that a new people had joined the community of nations. It was an era of vigorous, even boisterous, "Americanism."

The American character

Out of the great democratic surge came a widespread desire for social, economic, and political equality. Seemingly, every man aspired to be a member of the middle class. Certainly no one would admit that he belonged to the masses, and few would openly claim aristocratic origins. To dramatize the quest for the ordinary, it became fashionable to denounce the inequalities of other systems of government. Monarchy, for example, was regarded as a decadent relic of antiquity, based upon custom and privilege, and thoroughly out of date. Although Americans would sometimes boast privately that their family origins could be traced to high places in the old country, they saw nothing inconsistent in sneering at the institution of royalty. It was the democratic thing to do.

The cult of equalitarianism was a source of constant surprise to foreign visitors in America. Outwardly the citizens of the great democracy tended to look much alike in their dress. The similarity arose perhaps more because of the fact that in this country there were as yet no real extremes of poverty or wealth, rather than from any studied desire for sartorial democracy. However, the situation must have helped the people of lower income brackets feel that they had no decided superiors.

Along with this insistence upon personal equality there appeared a sentiment that seemed to run counter to it. The desire to achieve some kind of rank, to set oneself off from one's fellows, was everywhere. Coats of arms, reminiscent of European royalty, not only flourished but were so garishly elaborate that the self-respecting aristocrat on the other side of the Atlantic would have been embarrassed to have anything similar. Honorary titles were eagerly sought. Villages were overrun with men called Cap, Colonel, or Judge. A flabbergasted European visitor told of one small town where a local dignitary known as The General earned his title by his ability to train animals. Another observer found a fellow who was called The Judge because he was such a fine connoisseur of wines. Perhaps there was really nothing inconsistent in all this if one takes the point of view that in America democracy was so completely accepted that almost anyone could earn such "rank." Its achievement did not rest upon aristocratic blood, family origins, or privilege. Any village lad could make the grade by an earnest application of effort.

CORCORAN GALLERY OF ART

INDIANS OF THE PLAINS

The first trappers and settlers who entered the vast grasslands of North America lying between the Mississippi River and the Rocky Mountains came upon a civilization that was both new and startling to them. They found the world of the American Plains Indians, a hunting people who roamed the West much as the nomads roamed the desert. Their camps were moved seasonally, sometimes to escape hostile neighbors, but more often to follow the great herds of buffalo that supplied them with their meat for food, skins for clothing, and bones to be made into tools and weapons. Living as they did in land where the open space was almost without limitation, the plains people developed highly individual religious beliefs that helped them to cope with their great, lonely world. They conquered the physical problems and the dangers involved in traveling vast distances by becoming accomplished horsemen and warriors without peer. When the white man began to settle in the West, the old life on the plains was doomed. The buffalo was new and exciting game for hunters from the East, and extinction of the herds meant starvation for the Indians. Most important of all, the life of a wandering people could not be limited by the boundaries of farmers and ranchers. With all the fury and skill at their command, the plains tribes fought the advance of the frontier in the 19th century, retreating step by step, until, in the end, they were defeated by the superior number and weapons of the white man, and their civilization was lost.

THE
WANDERING LIFE

A party of Sioux sets out for a new camp (above). Their possessions are loaded on their backs or dragged on travois, the carriers made of poles that are hitched to horses and dogs. Riding ahead of the column, scouting braves are on the lookout for enemies. Except for encampments during the harsh winter months, the Plains Indian tribes were always on the move.

A Sioux village or camp is seen at the right. The women are preparing hides outside their tepees. These paintings were made by George Catlin, who went to the plains in the 1830s to record Indian life.

THE BUFFALO HUNT

A buffalo hunter prepares to take aim. Often the Indians could not find a herd of buffalo, and then they had to live on the meat they had preserved either by pounding it into a pulp and mixing it with fat or by drying it in long thin strips in the sun.

The brave above hunts in the deep of winter on snowshoes, aided by his dogs. The buffalo hunt was more difficult for the Indians without horses, for the great herds moved swiftly across the open plains.

The wily hunters below, disguised in wolfskins, are stealing up on a herd of buffalo with their bows and arrows in hand. Because a man on foot usually could not outrun a buffalo, he had to outwit him.

TALK, TOYS, AND SPORT

Mandan Indian braves (above, left) meet to smoke and exchange stories. Their lodge, which had a domed, earthen roof, served as a home, storehouse, stable, and kennel.

Plains Indian children played with small toys like those above. The pinto pony, buffalo, and elk—as well as the brave— were familiar sights in their daily life.

Life was not all hunting and fighting for the young Indian braves. The Sioux at the left are playing the fast, rough Indian game that the French named lacrosse.

503

ARTISTS OF THE PLAINS

An Indian Horse Dance.

In the Apache skin painting above, a ceremony is performed around a campfire in recognition of a girl's puberty. The dancers are girls, women, and medicine men.

An Indian artist did the stylized picture (opposite) of a ritual horse dance performed by the plains people. The rider shown full-face wears a buffalo mask.

The Sioux medicine shield at the right is decorated with a staring buffalo head. The Plains Indians had exceptional natural ability as artists and craftsmen.

All of the Plains Indians followed ancient laws and ceremonies. At the tribal powwow above, the chief, in accordance with the custom of his people, will ask the advice of the tribal elders on a matter of importance to the whole tribe.

The Mandan below, standing in the center of a lodge roof, is invoking the aid of the gods in bringing rain for the crops of his tribe. The rain-making ritual was one of the most important magic rites practiced by the people of the plains.

SMITHSONIAN INSTITUTION

ANCIENT WAYS

The Blackfoot woman above wears a head-dress for the Sun Dance ritual practiced by most Plains Indians. The participants evoked mystical visions while swaying, shuffling, and, sometimes, practicing forms of self-torture. The medicine man at the left, also a member of the Blackfoot tribe, wore his headdress while attempting to cure injuries and illnesses with ancient chants, ceremonies, and potions.

OVERLEAF: Men of the Mandan Bull Society do their frenzied ritual dance in an attempt to draw the great buffalo herds closer to their village. Mandan women also had an organization for this purpose.

CHAPTER 18

OPENING OF THE WEST

The Lewis and Clark expedition, sponsored by Jefferson, was the most important official examination of the high plains and the Northwest before the War of 1812. The President's secretary, Captain Meriwether Lewis, had been instructed to "explore the Missouri River, and such principal streams of it as, by its course and communication with the waters of the Pacific Ocean . . . may offer the most direct and practicable water communication across the continent, for the purposes of commerce." Captain William Clark, the younger brother of famed George Rogers Clark, was invited to share the command of the exploring party.

Amid rumors that there were prehistoric mammoths wandering around the unknown region, and that somewhere in its wilds was a mountain of rock salt, 80 by 45 miles in extent, the two captains set out. The date was May 14, 1804. Their point of departure was the mouth of the Wood River, just across the Mississippi from

Ready with rifles to attack, an Indian war party watches a wagon train, heading west, as it passes through its territory.

the entrance of the Missouri River. After toiling up the Missouri all summer, the group wintered near the Mandan villages in the center of modern North Dakota. Resuming their journey in the spring of 1805, the men worked their way along the Missouri to its source and then crossed the mountains of western Montana and Idaho. Picking up a tributary of the Columbia River, they continued westward until they reached the Pacific Ocean, where they stayed until spring. Starting back early in 1806, they made the return journey safely, arriving at St. Louis in late September.

The long, hazardous trip excited the imagination of the American people and raised their interest in the West. Lewis and Clark brought back much new information, including the knowledge that the continent was wider than originally supposed. More specifically, they learned a good deal about river drainages and mountain barriers. They ended speculation that an easy coast-to-coast route existed via the Missouri-Columbia River systems, and their reports of the climate, the animals and birds, the trees and plants, and the natives of the West—though not

511

immediately published—were made available to men of science.

The drama of the Lewis and Clark venture so occupied the public's attention that other significant explorations of the West during the same period went almost unnoticed. In 1804, as Lewis and Clark ascended the Missouri, a group of adventurers, led by William Dunbar and a Philadelphia chemist named Dr. George Hunter, moved up the Red River. The presence of hostile Spanish troops discouraged them, but they reached and explored the Washita River before they turned back. The next spring, Thomas Freeman, accompanied by a scientist, an army captain, and 19 men, again attempted to trace the Red River to its source. They examined it for some 600 miles, but also ran into Spanish opposition and withdrew.

The best known of those who explored the Central and Western plains were Lieutenant Zebulon Montgomery Pike and Major Stephen H. Long. In the summer of 1806, Pike crossed the plains to the Rocky Mountains, where he saw the peak that today bears his name. The next spring he examined the Royal Gorge of the Arkansas River and ventured into the San Luis Valley to the west. He moved too far south and was picked up by

William Clark   Meriwether Lewis

Three boats and 43 persons headed up the Missouri from St. Louis on May 14, 1804, as Lewis and Clark began their exploration of the land bought from France in the Louisiana Purchase. The party met a band of friendly Flathead Indians at Ross's Hole, Montana, on September 4, 1805. The two explorers are seen at the far right.

Spanish soldiers, who charged him with trespassing. After a time in custody in Chihuahua, Mexico, where he was relieved of his notes and maps, he was escorted back to the United States border and handed over to American authorities. Fortunately he remembered enough of what he had seen to make a useful report of his travels.

In 1820, Major Long covered much the same ground, with the exception of the side trip into Spanish territory. With a handful of soldiers, he traveled to the Colorado Rockies, where he, too, found a peak to bear his name. Neither Pike nor Long made any startling discoveries, but they added to the growing body of knowledge about the Western plains. Long is best remembered for the report of one of his associates who said the country they crossed on their way to the mountains was "almost wholly unfit for cultivation." Out of that and similar writings came the concept of the Great American Desert—a general belief that the country west of the Mississippi could not support a farming population. It held back further popular interest in the area for many years.

Some two decades later, a youthful officer named John C. Fremont resumed government explorations of the West. In 1842, guided by Kit Carson and other trappers and hunters, he crossed the Continental Divide at South Pass, already discovered by fur traders, and then returned to Washington, D. C. The next year he again moved across South Pass and marched northward to Fort Hall, in modern Idaho. From there he explored the country along the Columbia River, after which he went south to Sutter's Fort (Sacramento) for the winter. Early in 1844 he was at Los Angeles, and from there he made his way east, to Santa Fe and St. Louis.

Explorers were not the only white men in the early West. Fur trappers, popularly called mountain men, roamed through the Rockies and the Western country, trapping beaver to send to the fur markets in St. Louis. A number of them, like Jedediah Smith, Jim Bridger, Tom Fitzpatrick, and the Sublette brothers, became well known to the public. But it was a businessman named John Jacob Astor, sitting in a New York office issuing orders in broken English, who was responsible for much of the new geographical knowledge that came from the fur frontier. Members of his Pacific Fur Company established themselves on the Columbia River in 1811, and though they were forced to abandon the area during the War of 1812, they brought back much information on the country between the Missouri and

The earliest eyewitness picture of Pawnee Indians, drawn by Samuel Seymour, was of an 1819 parley at Council Bluffs, Iowa.

514

the Pacific through which they had traveled or trapped. In 1822, Astor set up a western headquarters at St. Louis and sent men back up the Missouri River. His only real rival was the Rocky Mountain Fur Company, which provided violent opposition for a few years during the 1830s. Until the end of the beaver-pelt era, "King John" reigned supreme between St. Louis and Fort Benton, Montana.

Oregon fever

In the early 1820s, a member of Congress from Massachusetts advised his colleagues that "our natural boundary is the Pacific Ocean. The swelling tide of our population must

roll on until that mighty ocean interposes its waters, and limits our territorial empire." Another Congressman agreed, stating that the government was powerless to prevent the spread of population to the Pacific Coast. This notion of the helplessness of man or government to stem the mighty tide of Western expansion gave rise to the term "manifest destiny." Many who used it were not wholly sure of its meaning, but they imagined that somewhere in the great unknown, a divine hand was guiding the destiny of American growth and that the movement was irrepressible.

In the next two decades, the manifest-destiny virus spread across the land. Residents of the Mississippi Valley became especially excited over the prospect that their region would become the take-off point for the next step west and that great profits would result from supplying hardy Americans who were venturing into unsettled regions. The possibilities stimulated a tremendous burst of patriotism on the part of tradesmen, not to mention land speculators and farmers with produce to sell.

By the early 1840s there were settlements in Arkansas, Missouri, Iowa, and Minnesota. Beyond them, the Great American Desert still seemed unsuited for settlers. But across the plains was Oregon, now popularly ac-

Jim Bridger   *John Charles Fremont*   *John Jacob Astor*

cepted as a rich, fertile country. This huge territory lay west of the Rockies, north of parallel 42 (modern California's northern border) and south of parallel 54°40′ (Alaska's southern boundary). At one time, four nations claimed it—Spain, Russia, Great Britain, and the United States. In 1819, Spain relinquished her claim, and a few years later Russia followed, withdrawing to the 54°40′ parallel.

The two remaining claimants, the United States and Great Britain, were unable to agree upon an equitable division of the territory so, in 1818, they decided to hold it jointly. This was satisfactory when the only inhabitants were fur traders and Indians. But when American farmers began to talk of migrating to the new promised land,

Indians make their camp at the base of the towering Fremont Peak, named after the explorer who scaled it in 1842 on his expedition in Wyoming's Wind River Range.

as they did in the early 1840s, trouble arose.

What were the forces generating this new westward impulse? The common man was moved by favorable reports about Oregon from travelers, explorers, and missionaries and by a desire to better his economic condition. For generations the frontiersmen had believed that opportunities were greater just a little farther west, and the belief generally had proved to be sound. Now added to the personal incentive was the national eagerness to grow larger. The two elements combined to make an example of manifest destiny.

From a political standpoint, many American leaders encouraged the settlement of Oregon. It would "force the issue" with Great Britain and secure the region for the United States. The notion was proclaimed loudly by such Senators as Thomas Hart Benton of Missouri (the father-in-law of explorer John Fremont), who chafed at

517

Chimney Rock in Nebraska was one of the great landmarks along the Oregon Trail. Alfred Jacob Miller painted it in 1837.

Britain's joint occupation of the distant territory. On one occasion, Benton urged his colleagues to "let the emigrants go on and carry their rifles. We want 30,000 rifles in the valley of the Oregon; they will make all quiet there."

Several events helped to stimulate the migration. The panic of 1837 caused many a farmer to hope things might be better on new land. Favorable reports from the Willamette Valley further roused this hope. Then, in 1841, a Senate bill proposed the construction of a line of forts up the Missouri River and across the mountains to the mouth of the Columbia. It also provided for Oregon land grants to male immigrants over 18 years of age. Although the bill was lost in the House, such legislative activity suggested a deep interest on the part of the federal government in encouraging families to head west. People generally believed that next time the bill might pass.

The idea was enough to cause an epidemic of Oregon fever. In 1843, hundreds of prairie schooners moved out along the Platte River route, well known since the day of the fur traders, to mark off what was to be called the Oregon Trail. There were more wagons the next year. In 1845, some 3,000 men, women, and children migrated, almost doubling Oregon's population in a single travel season.

The occupation of Oregon by settlers made the question of its ownership urgent. The United States had repeatedly suggested dividing the territory at the 49th parallel, but the British government had held out for the Columbia River. The result had been a diplomatic stalemate, accompanied by American threats that now grew in intensity.

Texas—three times refused

Oregon was not the only land coveted by American farmers. The panic of 1819 made a good many farmers anxious to leave the Mississippi Valley and put their troubles and debts behind them. Spanish Texas looked attractive. In 1812, Moses Austin obtained a land grant from the defunct government of New Spain, but died before he could carry out his plan of colonization. His son Stephen carried on and in 1822 received confirmation of his father's grant from the newly independent Mexican government. By 1825, young Austin's colony in Texas had a population of some 1,400 whites and over 400 slaves.

The American government was also interested in Texas. In August, 1829, President Jackson tried to buy it from Mexico for $5,000,000, but was turned down. Continued talk about acquiring the territory gradually aroused Mexican suspicions and made life hard for the colonists who had settled there. In time, the Mexican government began to pass restrictive legislation, limiting the number of American settlers in the area.

The climax came in March, 1836, when the Texans, led by Sam Houston, declared their independence. Prospects turned dark after the Texas garrison at the Alamo was wiped out, but on April 21, Houston and his volunteers defeated the Mexicans along the San Jacinto River and captured their leader, Santa Anna.

Although the now-independent Texans objected strenuously to outside control.—from Mexico or any other authority—many of them wanted annexation by the United States. Sup-

A group of tenderfoot immigrants to the West, camped down for the night, sit and listen intently to the veteran trapper as he tries to explain what lies ahead.

posedly this was exactly what the federal government had wanted also, as it had repeatedly tried to buy Texas from Mexico. But Mexico did not recognize Texas' independence, and Andrew Jackson now became hesitant, concerned that annexation might split his party as well as involve the country in war. His successor, Martin Van Buren, adopted the same policy, and in the fall of 1838, the Texans, with feelings hurt, withdrew their application for annexation, asserting they no longer wanted to be in the Union.

The pique lasted only a few years. By 1843, Santa Anna was again threatening war against the Texans, and Great Britain, presuming to use its influence to prevent a conflict, showed an interest in the matter that worried the American State Department. President John Tyler, who had succeeded to office in 1841 at the death of William Henry Harrison, renewed negotiations with Texas for annexation.

Early in April, 1844, an annexation treaty was finally signed and sent to the Senate for ratification. Then another road block appeared. John C. Calhoun, a leader of Southern proslavery forces, was the new Secretary of State. When he presented the treaty on a sectional basis, suggesting that the inclusion of Texas in the Union was necessary to maintain the South's "peculiar institution," there was a violent reaction. As Marquis James wrote, "Had he turned loose a wildcat amid that decorous company, the result would have been much the same."

The proposal was soundly rejected.

Sam Houston, once again the Texas President, had warned his old friend Andrew Jackson that another rebuff to his people would be serious. He compared Texas to a bride "adorned for her espousals" and predicted that if "she should be rejected, her mortification would be indescribable." As this was the third time the bride-to-be had said yes, such a sentiment was understandable. But now the Senate had once more left the bride standing at the altar. It appeared as if only a miracle could save the romance.

The politics of expansion

The failure of the federal government's courtship of Texas threw the matter into the hands of the electorate. Not long after the Senate's action, both political parties assembled to nominate candidates for the election of 1844. Jackson, old and ailing but still the titular head of his party, had not lost his yearning for possession of Texas. Passing over a surprised Martin Van Buren, who had declared himself against annexation, Old Hickory came out for the relatively unknown James K. Polk. The Whigs, who did not plan to make the Texas question an election issue, nominated Henry Clay, an annexation opponent. They were confident that their candidate, celebrated as he was, would have little trouble beating the Democratic unknown from Tennessee.

Polk, the dark horse, used an old but effective device—a catchy cam-

Sam Houston   Stephen Austin   Antonio Lopez de Santa Anna

Austin brought the settlers into Texas in 1821, but it was not until Houston defeated Santa Anna at San Jacinto in 1836 that they won their freedom from Mexico.

paign slogan. Soon he and his followers had thousands of voters echoing "The Reoccupation of Oregon and the Reannexation of Texas." To this cry was added "54° 40′ or fight," meaning that the United States should take "All of Oregon or none," to quote another popular phrase.

The Democrats had enough political sagacity to capitalize upon a trend. Realizing that manifest destiny was running strong, they rode it to victory. "Harry of the West" managed to get only 105 electoral votes to Polk's 170. Apparently the voters approved enlarging the nation's territorial holdings. To Polk the mandate was clear.

The President-elect was to have part of his political harvest snatched away, however. The incumbent, John Tyler, wished to bring the Republic of Texas into the Union himself. He was faced by the difficult fact that the Senate had rejected the proposal and would surely repeat the insult if given a chance. There were just not enough pro-Texas votes for the necessary two-thirds. In December, 1844, Tyler proposed to Congress that a joint resolution, requiring only a simple majority of both Houses, be voted upon. The maneuver worked. The resolution passed the House easily, and squeaked by the Senate, 27 to 25. On March 1—three days before he left office—Tyler signed the resolution and at once notified Texas that it had been invited to become the 28th state.

When Polk was inaugurated, the annexation of Texas was practically complete, but another matter faced him. The campaign had raised threats of "54° 40′ or fight" over Oregon. Because this had been something of

521

an election promise, he felt obliged to fulfill his party's campaign plank. He grumbled about it in his diary: "The truth is that in all this Oregon discussion in the Senate, too many Democratic Senators have been more concerned about the Presidential election in '48 than they have about settling Oregon, whether at 49° or 54°40'." But Polk was President, and the party leader. It was up to his administration to bring about some kind of settlement.

In 1846, the British indicated that they were ready to resolve the Oregon question if it could be done fairly. Polk wanted neither "54°40'" nor "fight," but how to compromise without losing face? At length he hit upon asking the Senate's advice. When that body agreed to the British suggestion of the 49th parallel, the President "reluctantly" accepted their opinion, assuming the attitude of being forced into the concession. On June 15, 1846, the Senate ratified the treaty, and the boundary was continued along parallel 49° from the Rockies to the Pacific Ocean. Oregon was "reoccupied."

Golden California

With Texas and Oregon in the fold, Americans now looked longingly at another part of the Pacific Coast— the Mexican province of California. Again Polk went along with public opinion, and when it was rumored that Great Britain had designs on that part of the continent, he believed it as quickly as the next man. Without hesitation he ordered a program of in- filtrating California by appointing Thomas O. Larkin as his secret agent to foment revolt among California Mexicans. At the same time, he made it clear to Mexico that he would pay as high as $40,000,000 for the province.

But Mexico showed no inclination to sell. In 1835, Andrew Jackson had tried without success to buy San Francisco Bay for half a million dollars; now, a decade later, Polk was faced with the same resistance in his attempt to buy all of California. Baring his frustration before Congress, he declared that the people of the North American continent should have the right to decide their own destiny and promised protection from foreign interference to any independent state seeking entrance into the Union. He could not have made his position much clearer to those who were sewing their crude bear flags out beyond the towering Sierras.

On June 10, 1846, a group of settlers, dressed in greasy buckskins and wearing the mantle of manifest destiny, touched off the California bid for independence by stealing a band of General Jose Castro's horses. That they meant rebellion and not robbery was made plain a few days later when another group captured the prominent Mariano Vallejo and hauled him off to Sutter's Fort, despite his protestations that he favored peaceful acquisition of California by the Americans.

The uprising of the Californians was hastily improvised. Some of the Americans in the province attached themselves to the small command of John C. Fremont, who was in California on one of his expeditions of Western exploration. Other Americans made for Monterey and San Francisco, where United States ships provided naval aid. By July, the word had spread that the United States and Mexico were at war—a fact that permitted the Stars and Stripes to be raised over California localities with less embarrassment. Fremont's forces swept southward, meeting almost no resistance. On August 17, Commodore Robert F. Stockton announced at Los Angeles, "The flag of the United States is now flying from every commanding position in the Territory, and California is entirely free from Mexican domination." It was almost true. In September, a counterrevolution started in southern California that was not stamped out until mid-January, 1847.

A few weeks later, General Stephen Watts Kearny, who had marched his men across the Southwest to participate in the climax of hostilities, was formally installed as military governor. The manifest-destiny map makers had added another piece to their growing territorial mosiac and had pushed the westward-moving American frontier to the Pacific Ocean.

The Mexican War, formally terminated in February, 1848, gave final confirmation to the acquisition of California. Just a few days before the

A supply train, moving slowly across the desert to bring provisions to settlers who are farther west, is put into desperate flight by an Indian attack.

Treaty of Guadalupe Hidalgo was signed, an event occurred in the foothills of central California that would have made the Mexican signatories groan with dismay had they known of it. One of John Sutter's employees, James Marshall, found gold on the south fork of the American River while building a sawmill. This brought gold seekers from everywhere, and the human avalanche upon California was so great that the region was catapulted into statehood almost overnight. Bypassing the usual territorial stage of initiation, it entered the fraternity of states as part of the Compromise of 1850.

The Great Medicine Road

The tramping feet of men and beasts, westward bound, hammered out trails that later became roads and finally highways. Among the more important were the Santa Fe Trail angling across Missouri, Kansas, and southeastern Colorado to the ancient Spanish town that gave the trail its name; the Smoky Hill Passage across Kansas to the Colorado mines; and the Great Medicine Road, as the Indians called it, between the Missouri River and the West. The Great Medicine Road had several names. The Oregon immigrants had moved over it—out along the Platte, across present Wyoming and southern Idaho, to the Columbia River. The Mormons had followed them, in a general way, swinging down along the Green River and past Jim Bridger's establishment on Black's

Fork en route to the Salt Lake Valley. Then the California Argonauts had come, retracing the Mormons' steps and striking out across the bleakness that lay west of Salt Lake City in the hope of reaching the watercourses of the Sierras alive. So the roadway had become the Oregon Trail, the California Trail, or just the Great Western Road.

After the pioneers came stage lines, wagon-freighting companies, then the Union Pacific and Central Pacific Railroads, and finally automobile highways US 30 and 40 overlaid by Interstate 80 and 70. But long before the days of the superhighway, this main route west was well known to Americans. There were highly romanticized accounts of the ordeals of making the journey. A familiar image of the Oregon Trail in its heyday is of white-topped prairie schooners tightly circled, tongue to tailgate, surrounded by galloping savages, howling and dealing out death with their government-issue rifles. The more common hazards were just as deadly but less dramatic. Cholera killed more immigrants than did the Indians. Sicknesses of all kinds, accidents, malnutrition, and thirst caused the greatest hardships. Once the road was fairly well established, however, the risks diminished, and it was only a matter of time and boredom between the Missouri River and a Western destination.

As travel increased, way stations grew in number along various routes, and from these sprang small, isolated

Fort Laramie, Wyoming, on the North Platte River, was a fur-trading post and rendezvous for trappers and Indians until 1849, when the army took it over.

communities. Some of the settlements became important and demanded better communication with "the States." One of them was the Mormon center in Salt Lake Valley. As early as 1850, Samuel Woodson of Independence, Missouri, received a contract to carry the mail to the Mormons. He agreed to establish a monthly service across 1,200 miles of parched wilderness for approximately $20,000 a year. Up the Platte River route, past Fort Kearny, Nebraska, beyond Fort Laramie, to Jim Bridger's outpost went the mail-

bags. From there to Salt Lake City the going was easier. A few years later, when stagecoach service was established, the mail was delivered weekly and travel time was reduced from a month to 18 days.

The Overland Trail ran through the hunting grounds of the Plains Indians, and in 1849 the government responded to appeals for protection on the road by garrisoning Fort Laramie. It was not enough. To placate the Indians' growing restlessness, commissioners met with them at the fort in 1851. In

The only known interior view of the original Fort Laramie, painted in 1837 by Alfred Jacob Miller, shows fur-trading Indians assembled in small groups.

this largest and most important meeting of its kind in the West, the tribes promised, in return for annuities and protection from the immigrants, not to molest travelers on the trail. But the council signalized the beginning of the end for the plains tribes. Before long, miners and settlers would overrun the countryside, paying no heed to Indian rights.

One of the outcomes of the Laramie Treaty was the establishment of a number of military posts along the great road. It resulted, in turn, in more traffic by men and vehicles sup-

plying the soldiers who guarded the route. And sometimes the blue-clad watchmen were overzealous. They took their duties so seriously that they brought on trouble where there was none before. A good example was the conduct of impulsive young Lieutenant J. L. Grattan, fresh from West Point and eager to make a name for himself at Fort Laramie. In the late summer of 1854, not long after the lieutenant had first come west, several bands of the Sioux were camped along the North Platte in the vicinity of the fort. On August 18, a cow wandered from a group of Scandinavian Mormons who were passing by, and the Indians killed it.

Several of the Sioux journeyed to Fort Laramie and reported the incident to the post commander, who requested Grattan to investigate. He set out at once with an intoxicated interpreter, a few mounted men, a wagonload of infantrymen, and two cannons, determined to bring back the offending Indian or Indians. At the Sioux camp there was a brief argument followed by threats, and then shooting. No white man survived the encounter, and the lieutenant's corpse, bristling like a porcupine with 24 arrows in it, was identified only with difficulty. An Indian agent who arrived at Fort Laramie shortly after the slaughter said that more reasonable conduct by the hotheaded army officer would have prevented bloodshed. In fact, he understood that the Indians had offered to pay for the cow, but the manner in which the negotiations were carried out had not given them the opportunity to make the offer to the lieutenant and his interpreter.

The Grattan massacre, as it was called, was followed by Indian raids on immigrant trains and freight convoys. These scattered attacks, together with a general sullenness among the Northern tribes, prompted the federal government to take punitive measures. Colonel William S. Harney moved out of Fort Kearny, Nebraska, in the summer of 1855 with 600 men and the loud announcement, "By God, I'm for battle—no peace." The colonel had his wish. There was battle, and there was no peace. The Indian wars were just beginning.

Meanwhile, traffic on the Medicine Road was becoming heavier. In May, 1857, some 2,500 federal troops under the command of Colonel Albert Sidney Johnston (who would, a few years later, die at Shiloh, wearing the Confederate gray) marched to Utah to quell rebellious Mormons. To the firm of Russell, Majors, and Wadell went contracts for supplying the soldiery. Here was a freighting organization with enough equipment of its own literally to supply an army: In 1858, it owned 3,500 wagons and 40,000 draft animals and had in its employ about 4,000 men. Horace Greeley, making a Western visit in 1859, was deeply impressed by the size of the company's operations: "Such acres of wagons! Such pyramids of extra axletrees! Such herds of oxen! Such regiments of drivers and other employees! No one who does not see can realize how vast a business this is, nor how immense is its outlay as well as its income. I presume this great firm has at this hour two millions of dollars invested in stock, mainly oxen, mules, and wagons." This was the scene at Leavenworth, Kansas. Although such a collection of transportation equipment was unusual, there were many smaller overland freighters at other starting points. Collectively they amounted to an enormous army, poised along the Missouri River, for

Brigham Young

*On April 9, 1847, the Mormon pioneers
set out on the Oregon Trail to journey to
the valley of the Great Salt Lake. Here
they move into camp for the night, gather
buffalo chips, and then light their fires.*

the economic invasion of the West.

Trouble with the Mormons had
stemmed from the Mexican War.
When they moved into the Great
Basin, they thought they were moving
out of the United States, only to have
the Treaty of Guadalupe Hidalgo
thrust them back into it. By 1850,
what is now Utah and most of Nevada, as well as some of present western Colorado and a bit of Wyoming,
had become Utah Territory, with
Brigham Young as governor. Difficulties between the governor and his appointed officials, especially the judi-
ciary, led to a threat of civil violence
in the new Zion. To halt the unrest,
and perhaps to help take the nation's
mind off the mounting slave crisis in
the South, President Buchanan fired

Brigham Young and dispatched Colonel Johnston to Utah.

Winter overtook the slow-moving
troops, obliging them to hole up at
Fort Bridger until the weather moder-
ated, and thus provided time for a
peaceful settlement. In the summer of
1858, troops marched into Salt Lake

528

City peacefully, rebellious Mormons were pardoned, and the affair passed into history. Buchanan's bluff had cost the government about $15,000,000, much of which went into transport and supply for the expedition.

The Utah affair was concluded on the eve of the Civil War. Nearly six decades after the Louisiana Purchase, the trans-Mississippi West was still under examination by its new owners, and those who lived in it—both red and white—were restless and insecure. It was the postwar generation that settled the destiny of this vast part of the American Republic.

MAIN TEXT CONTINUES IN VOLUME 7

530

Jedediah S. Smith:
Unsung Pathfinder of the West

A SPECIAL CONTRIBUTION BY

STEPHEN W. SEARS

At the age of 23, carrying a rifle and a Bible, Smith went into the Northwest Territory, and within five years was one of the best and most courageous explorers of unknown lands.

At the port of San Diego in December, 1826, Captain William Cunningham, master of the ship *Courier* out of Boston, recorded, "There has arrived at this place Capt. Jedediah Smith with a company of hunters, from St. Louis, on the Missouri. . . . Does it not seem incredible that a party of 14 men, depending entirely upon their rifles and traps for subsistence, will explore this vast continent, and call themselves happy when they can obtain the tail of a beaver to dine upon?"

The captain had witnessed the completion of the first overland journey to California, led by a fellow Yankee just 27 years old. This in itself was a solid achievement, but Jed Smith during a seven-year odyssey also found South Pass, the historic gateway to the Far West; discovered the arid vastness of the Great Basin; grasped the existence of the Sierra Nevada mountain barrier to California and made the initial crossing of that imposing range; and, finally, was the first white man to traverse virtually the entire length of Amer-

While no likeness of Jedediah Smith exists, artist Harvey Dunn has captured the strength and spirit of the famous trapper and explorer.

ica's Pacific coast, from southern California to the Columbia River in Oregon.

Jedediah Smith, not John C. Fremont, ought to be remembered today as the West's pathfinder. Yet his name never became impressed upon the American consciousness. Only recently has research by Western historians, particularly Maurice Sullivan and Dale Morgan, restored Jedediah Strong Smith to the first rank of America's explorers.

Arriving in St. Louis early in 1822 at the age of 23, Jed Smith sought a career in the mountains at precisely the moment when the long-restrained American assault on the Western fur trade burst loose. The depression following the War of 1812 had subsided, venture capital was again available, and the vicious Blackfeet Indians showed signs of being amenable.

Unfortunately, almost nothing was known of what lay on the far side of the Rocky Mountains. There was supposed to be a huge inland sea and a series of major westward-flowing rivers, especially the fabled Buenaventura. The headwaters of the Missouri and the far Northwest contained beaver in quantity. Why not the valleys of those mighty rivers of the West?

Jed Smith was later to write of his motives for going to St. Louis in 1822, "I started into the mountains with the determination of becoming a first-rate hunter, of making myself thoroughly acquainted with the character and habits of the Indians, of tracing out the sources of the Columbia River and following it to its mouth." To which he added, because he was a

531

New England Yankee at heart, "and of making the whole profitable to me."

Smith was born in 1799 of New England parents in what is now Bainbridge, New York. The family drifted westward to Erie County and later to Ohio's Western Reserve. Coming of age, Jedediah struck out for the frontier.

William H. Ashley, lieutenant governor of Missouri, was eager for a share in the fur-trade riches. In partnership with Andrew Henry, Ashley advertised for "Enterprising Young Men to ascend the river Missouri to its source." Smith quickly signed on and spent his first mountain winter with one of Henry's trapping parties high up the Missouri. In the spring, Henry dispatched him to tell Ashley to bring more horses.

Pulling up the Missouri with supplies, the party stopped to trade for horses with the Arikara Indians. Instead of trade, they got bullets. Smith and the shore party were pinned under a murderous fire, and before they could escape, 12 were dead and 11 wounded, two of them mortally.

Jed Smith hastened to Henry's outpost with the news, then returned to serve in a punitive military expedition against the Arikaras. Ashley's loss was considerable, but at least the Missouri artery was open again.

For the fall beaver hunt, Smith was given his first command. It was a party of exceptional quality, including Thomas Fitzpatrick, Jim Clyman, William Sublette, Thomas Eddie, and Edward Rose, all of whom became famous mountain men in their own right. They set off due west from the Missouri toward the Dakota Badlands and the Black Hills, breaking a new trail to the mountains. At one point, Smith was attacked by the mountain men's dreaded enemy, a grizzly bear. Clyman has left a description of the encounter: "Grissly did not hesitate a moment but sprang on the cap't. taking him by the head first pitc[h]ing [him]

sprawling on the earth . . . breaking several of his ribs and cutting his head badly. . . . The bear had taken nearly all his head in his capa[c]ious mouth close to his left eye on one side and clos to his right ear on the other and laid the skull bare to near the crown of the head. . . . One of his ears was torn from his head out to the outer rim."

Under Smith's cool direction, Clyman some-

532

how stitched up the gaping wounds, even sav-
ing the ear.

The trappers plunged on into the Rockies,
taking beaver and wintering with a tribe of
friendly Crow Indians. On the spring hunt of
1824, they found a practical way west through
the Divide via the wide gap of South Pass, and
set about trapping the beaver-rich Green River
Valley. Instructing Fitzpatrick to report these

developments to Ashley, Smith and six of his
men plunged deep into the mountains to the
northwest.

Fitzpatrick's report of South Pass and the
rich Green River Valley convinced Ashley
to try and recoup his loss on the Missouri. He
made the difficult march to the Green River,
arriving in April, 1825, and set about trap-

ping—but under a new system. His instructions read, "The place of deposite, as aforesaid, will be the place of rendavoze for all our parties on or before the 10th July next." Thus was born the effective rendezvous system that became the cornerstone of the American fur trade. No longer need the mountain man make the annual trek to civilization with his furs. Now supply caravans would come to him, buy his pelts, and sell to him in return—at astronomical prices—the supplies he needed to be self-sufficient the year round. The rendezvous became a wild carnival of gambling, races, monumental drunks, cavorting Indians, wenching, and storytelling, and the typical trapper

left it hung over and broke to return to his lonely beaver streams.

Smith was at that first rendezvous (quiet by later standards), where the logistics of the new practice were worked out. Andrew Henry had passed from the trade, and Smith became Ashley's new partner. A year later, he, William Sublette and David E. Jackson bought out Ashley. Jedediah Smith, after just four years in the mountains, became the senior partner of the firm that now dominated the American fur trade. He was 27.

The new partners realized that the beaver streams of the interior Rockies were becoming well enough known so that their productive

future was limited. But there were still those legendary rivers of the West hopefully thick with beaver, shown on the maps. Leaving Sublette and Jackson to handle matters in the mountains, Smith turned his face westward toward an unknown country.

In August of 1826 his party—the self-styled South West Expedition—rode along the Sevier River into what Smith called "a Country of Starvation—Sandy plains and Rocky Hills once in 20 30 or 40 m a little pond or Spring." Striking the Colorado at what is now Lake Mead, they followed it southward. On foot, their horses worn out, they fi-

nally reached a haven in the Mojave villages not far from today's Needles, California. The expedition had so far found no beaver and no Buenaventura River coursing westward, and Smith determined to strike out for the coast.

It took two painful weeks to cross the blazing Mojave Desert, but at length they gained California's San Bernardino Valley, where they found a warm welcome at San Gabriel Mission. Smith's clerk, Harrison Rogers, described

535

*This trapper, alone in wild country, is vulner-
able, as Smith often was, to Indians and animals.*

it: "Great feasting among the men. . . . I was
introduced to the 2 Priests over a glass of good
old whiskey—and found them to be very joval
friendly gentlemen. . . . Plenty of good wine
during supper, before the cloth was removed
sigars was introduced. . . . Friendship and
peace prevail with us and the Spanyards." In
the spring of 1827, Smith headed into the San
Joaquin Valley. He still sought the Buenaventura, hoping it would lead him to the
summer rendezvous near Great Salt Lake.

He drove northward some 350 miles, but
the looming presence of the Sierra Nevada
formed a constant barrier to the east. There
was no Buenaventura River. The 15-man party
and its equipment was too cumbersome to
cross the icy, snow-covered range. Leaving
most of his men behind to trap the waters of
the Stanislaus River, Smith set out with two
companions, Robert Evans and Silas Gobel.
They made the historic crossing of the Sierra,
skirted Walker Lake, and struck out into
central Nevada.

Smith's journal leaves a picture of the desert
journey: "I could discover nothing but sandy
plains or dry Rocky hills. . . . Worn down with

hunger and fatigue and burning with thirst increased by the blazing sands . . . it then seemed
possible and even probable we might perish in
the desert unheard of and unpitied. . . . My
dreams were not of Gold or ambitious honors
but of my distant quiet home, of murmuring
brooks, of Cooling Cascades."

Evans collapsed, and Smith and Gobel
pressed on to find water. Smith returned with
a kettle full. "Putting the kettle to his mouth,
Evans did not take it away until he had drank
4 or 5 quarts and then asked me why I had not
brought more."

At last they sighted Great Salt Lake and
passed along its southern shore. To cross the
flooded Jordan River, Smith cobbled together
a raft for their belongings. Holding the tow-
rope in his teeth, with Evans and Gobel hanging onto the raft, he swam them across. On
July 3, 1827, having covered over 600 miles in
six weeks, most of it on foot, the three men
reached the rendezvous at Bear Lake, on the
Utah-Idaho border. Smith laconically re-
marked that "my arrival caused a considerable
bustle in camp, for myself and party had been
given up as lost."

While Sublette and Jackson had done well,
putting the new firm on a solid footing,
Jed Smith was concerned about his own party
stranded in California. Ten days after his arrival, he was headed southwest again with 18
men. Generally following the same route as
the previous fall, they reached the Mojave
Indian villages, but this time it was no haven.

The Mojaves had tangled painfully with
trappers from Taos, and as the Americans
crossed the Colorado, the vengeful Indians
struck without warning. With eight survivors,
Smith took refuge in a copse of cottonwoods,
opened fire, and "the indians ran off like
frightened sheep." Nonetheless, the situation
was critical. All the horses and provisions, except 15 pounds of dried meat, were gone; to
defend themselves, they had only their knives
and five guns. There was no choice but to
cross the desert on foot.

They reached the San Bernardino Valley in
late August, and immediately moved north to
rejoin the party left on the Stanislaus, arriving

just two days ahead of the September 20 deadline Smith had set for his return.

Nothing had gone right so far, and Jed Smith's luck continued bad. Seeking supplies at San Jose Mission, his welcome was in sharp contrast to that described by Harrison Rogers the previous fall at San Gabriel. He was ordered to leave the territory by the military commandant at San Francisco. He sold his beaver skins and bought 250 horses and mules, which he intended to drive to the mountain rendezvous hundreds of miles to the east, where he might sell them at a 400% profit.

The previous year his California explorations had touched on the Sacramento River, and local rumor had it that its upper reaches angled northeast through the Sierra Nevada. Perhaps here was the Buenaventura at last—a navigable connection with the Columbia River system and a new route to the Rockies bypassing the deserts and salt plains. But the Sacramento was not the Buenaventura, and the northern California wilderness proved incredibly difficult to drive horses through. The heavy rains were constant and the geography confusing. Marauding Indians shot ar-

Frederic Remington painted this impression of Smith. He is shown, in 1826, leading his party of 17 men across the barren Mojave Desert to the Mexican territory of California.

rows into the herd, Smith was kicked by a mule and "hurt pretty bad," and Rogers was seriously mauled by a grizzly. Rogers' entry in his journal for May 22, 1828, reads, "Oh! God, may it please thee . . . to still guide, & protect us, through this wilderness of doubt & fear."

On July 14, the 19-man party was at the Umpqua River, halfway up the Oregon coast, and Smith and two men went ahead to scout. Two days previously they had disciplined a Kelawatset chief for stealing an axe, but now Rogers, left in charge of the camp, apparently felt secure because they were in well-ordered Hudson's Bay territory. He admitted a large number of Kelawatset tribesmen to the camp, and the Indians murderously avenged their chief's insult. Only one of the 16 men escaped. Smith, his two companions, and the lone survivor of the massacre managed to make their way on foot to the British Hudson's Bay Company base at Fort Vancouver on the Columbia, 100 miles to the north.

The destitute Smith was welcomed by Dr. John McLoughlin, who ruled the Columbia district for the company. McLoughlin immediately dispatched an expedition to reinforce discipline and try to recover the goods of his erstwhile competitor. Smith went with them and they gathered what they could—a few horses, part of the furs, a handful of guns and utensils, and, fortunately for history, the journals of Smith and Rogers. McLoughlin generously gave Smith a fair price for his horses and skins, and in return, Smith filled McLoughlin in on his extensive discoveries and made him a map that must have straightened out a prodigious amount of geographic confusion.

By August, 1829, Smith had rejoined his two partners in Montana, and during the next year they trapped with success the upper Missouri region and the Yellowstone and its tributaries. But Jed Smith had had his fill of the sudden death and desperate loneliness of the wilderness. At the rendezvous of 1830, he and his partners sold out, and Smith was able to return to St. Louis a moderately wealthy man, only eight years after first going there.

Knowing the West better than any man alive, he began to prepare his invaluable journals and maps for publication. But, fatefully, he invested in and joined a trading caravan to Santa Fe that left St. Louis in April, 1831. It should have been a routine journey, but the train went astray in the arid plain between the Arkansas and Cimarron Rivers and ran short of water. As he had done countless times before, Smith set out alone to find it, and the final tragedy overtook him.

The story was later pieced together from the accounts of Indian traders. Smith found water, but was trapped by a hostile Comanche war party. The violent, one-sided encounter was quickly over, but the Comanche chief died with him. The date was May 27, 1831, and Jed Smith was just 32 years old.

An anonymous eulogist wrote that "though he fell under the spears of the savages, and his body glutted the prairie wolf, and none can tell where his bones are bleaching, he must not be forgotten." But he *was* forgotten. Unaccountably, no one stepped forward to preserve or publish his work, and the journals and letters and maps were either destroyed by fire or simply dropped from sight.

His biographer, Dale Morgan, calls Smith "an authentic American hero," and it is a judgment hard to fault. Tall and wiry, blue-eyed, clean-shaven, of devout faith and high intelligence, Jed Smith was a breed apart from most of his wild-living, amoral compatriots. But he did have, in abundant measure, all of the mountain man's skills. He earned the grudging respect of his competitors and something much like awe among those who followed him. He had the sort of wide-ranging, inquiring mind that marks all great explorers. He even found time to send seeds gathered on his travels to a botanist friend.

The exploits of this remarkable man make it unlikely that such a heroic image will ever tarnish. This seems only fair, for Jedediah Smith, so quickly forgotten in his own time, certainly deserves to be remembered in ours.

Stephen W. Sears has contributed to American Heritage Magazine *and is the editor of the* American Heritage Junior Library Series.

FOR FURTHER READING

CHAPTER 16

The American Heritage Book of the Pioneer Spirit. New York: 1959. An illustrated study of the impact of frontier life upon the history of the United States.

Andrist, Ralph K. *The California Gold Rush.* New York: American Heritage (Junior Library), 1961. The story of the discovery of gold in California, with contemporary illustrations

Billington, Ray A. *Westward Expansion.* New York: Macmillan, 1949. A detailed examination of the history of the American frontier.

DeVoto, Bernard A. *The Year of Decision, 1846.* Boston: Little, Brown, 1943. What happened on the Far Western pre-Civil War frontier.

Kirkland, Edward C. *A History of American Economic Life.* New York: F. S. Crofts, 1932. Chapter 4 discusses the importance of agriculture to the West.

Paxson, Frederic Logan. *A History of the American Frontier: 1763–1893.* Boston: Houghton Mifflin, 1924.

Place, Marian T. *Westward on the Oregon Trail.* New York: American Heritage (Junior Library), 1962. The story of the first great roadway to the Pacific slope.

Riegel, Robert E. *America Moves West.* New York: Henry Holt, 1930. The most readable general treatment of the frontier.

Turner, Frederick Jackson. *The Frontier in American History.* New York: Henry Holt, 1920. The classic study of the importance of the frontier to the American way of life and one of the books that has most influenced thinking on the history of the United States.

CHAPTER 17

Curti, Merle. *The Growth of American Thought.* New York: Harpers, 1943. Chapters 10 and 11 are pertinent to the material discussed in this volume.

Gabriel, Ralph. *The Course of American Democratic Thought.* New York: Ronald Press, 1940. The development in American intellectual history since 1815.

Mathiessen, F. O. *American Renaissance.* New York: Oxford University Press, 1941. A detailed study of language and thought in the age of Emerson.

Parrington, Vernon L. *Main Currents in American Thought.* 3 volumes. New York: Harcourt, Brace, 1927–30. One of the basic books on the development of the American attitude toward freedom, emphasizing the growth of the liberal tradition.

Tyler, Alice Felt. *Freedom's Ferment: Phases of American Social History to 1860.* Minneapolis: University of Minnesota Press, 1944. The religious and reform movements of the early Republic are presented as twin manifestations of the desire to perfect human institutions.

CHAPTER 18

Athearn, Robert G. *High Country Empire: The High Plains and the Rockies.* New York: McGraw-Hill, 1960. A detailed regional history.

Hafen, Le Roy, and Carl Coke Rister. *Western America.* New York: Prentice-Hall, 1941. The development of the Western United States.

Jones, Evan. *Trappers and Mountain Men.* New York: American Heritage (Junior Library), 1961. The story of the trappers who discovered and settled many sections of the United States.

Kraenzel, Carl Frederick. *The Great Plains in Transition.* Norman: University of Oklahoma Press, 1955. A sociological study of the changes that took place on the Great Plains as the settlers came.

Rachlis, Eugene. *Indians of the Plains.* New York: American Heritage (Junior Library), 1960. The story of the Indians the settlers encountered on the plains.

THE AMERICAN HERITAGE NEW ILLUSTRATED HISTORY OF THE UNITED STATES

PUBLISHED BY DELL PUBLISHING CO., INC.

George T. Delacorte, Jr., *Publisher*   Helen Meyer, *President*
William F. Callahan, Jr., *Executive Vice-President*

Walter B. J. Mitchell, Jr., *Project Director;* Ross Claiborne, *Editorial Consultant;* William O'Gorman, *Editorial Assistant;* John Van Zwienen, *Art Consultant;* Rosalie Barrow, *Production Manager*

CREATED AND DESIGNED BY THE EDITORS OF AMERICAN HERITAGE MAGAZINE

James Parton, *Publisher;* Joseph J. Thorndike, Jr., *Editorial Director;* Bruce Catton, *Senior Editor;* Oliver Jensen, *Editor;* Richard M. Ketchum, *Editor, Book Division;* Irwin Glusker, *Art Director*

ROBERT R. ENDICOTT, *Project Editor-in-Chief*

James Kraft, *Assistant Editor;* Nina Page, Evelyn H. Register, Lynn Marett, *Editorial Assistants;* Lina Mainiero, *Copy Editor;* Murray Belsky, *Art Director;* Eleanor A. Dye, *Designer;* John Conley, *Assistant*